MW01147006

Overcoming Your Shadow Mission

Also by John Ortberg

OVERCOMING YOUR SHADOW MISSION

JOHN
ORTBERG

ZONDERVAN.com/
AUTHOR**TRACKER**
follow your favorite authors

Overcoming Your Shadow Mission
Copyright © 2008 by John Ortberg

Requests for information should be addressed to:
Zondervan, *Grand Rapids, Michigan 49530*

Library of Congress Cataloging-in-Publication Data

Ortberg, John.
   Overcoming your shadow mission / John Ortberg.
     p. cm. — (Leadership library)
   ISBN 978-0-310-28760-5 (hardcover)
   1. Bible. O.T. Esther—Criticism, interpretation, etc. 2. Vocation—Christianity—
Biblical teaching. I. Title.
   BS1375.52.O78 2008
   222'.906--dc22   2008012131

Portions of this book first appeared in *When the Game Is Over, It All Goes Back in the Box*, © John Ortberg, Grand Rapids, Mich.: Zondervan, 2007.

Interior design by CHANGE Design Group

Printed in the United States of America

08 09 10 11 12 13 14 • 10 9 8 7 6 5 4 3 2 1

LEADERSHIP LIBRARY

The purpose of the Leadership Library is to provide leaders in all arenas—churches, businesses, schools, or nonprofits—with the cutting-edge thinking and the practical advice they need to take their leadership skills to the next level.

Books in the Leadership Library reflect the wisdom and experience of proven leaders who offer big insights in a pocket-size package. Whether you read these books on your own or with a group of colleagues, the Leadership Library presents critical insight into today's leadership challenges.

This little book is most gratefully dedicated to

Jimmy "Protein Bar" Mellado

Dick "Rockford East" Anderson

Doug "Mr. Hand" Veenstra

Freddy "Three Napkins" Vojtsek

Nancy "No More Tears" Beach

Overcoming Your Shadow Mission

E verybody—every human being on earth—has a mission. We were all put here for a purpose. Organizations like businesses, churches, and schools have them too. Leaders love to think about mission, love to cast vision for the mission, love to strategize about mission, love to achieve mission, love to celebrate mission.

And everybody has a *shadow mission*. Our lives, and the lives of the groups we're part of, can drift into the pursuit of something unworthy and dark. To give in to our shadow mission is—or should be—our greatest fear. To overcome our shadow mission is what this book is about. But I'm getting ahead of the story.

A few years ago a friend talked me into going on one of those discover-the-wild-inner-hairy-warrior-within-you men's weekends. It was held at a remote and primitive quasi-military campground. I could tell you where it was, but then I'd have to kill you. We arrived in darkness. Silent men with flashlights who had watched *Apocalypse Now* once too often led us wordlessly to a processing room. Our duffel bags were searched, and all prohibited items (snacks, reading materials, signal flares) were confiscated. We were assigned numbers that were to be used instead of our names to identify us through most of the weekend.

We chanted. We marched unclad through the snow. For two days we ate bark and berries. We were sleep deprived. We howled at the moon. We sat on our haunches in a Chippewa warrior teepee/sauna purifying our souls in the glandular fellowship of sweat, thirty men evaporating in a space no more than six sane Chippewa warriors would have tried to crowd into.

But strangely enough, in the middle of all

the psychobabble and melodrama came moments of unforgettable insight. One of the topics we covered at this retreat was how we were created for a mission. This was familiar territory. Then one speaker said something that stuck with me. He said if we don't embrace our true mission, we will by default pursue what he called a "shadow mission"—patterns of thought and action based on temptations and our own selfishness that lead us to betray our deepest values. The result: regret and guilt.

He told us what his particular shadow mission consists of: "My shadow mission is to watch TV and masturbate while the world goes to hell."

His language was more raw than this, and a round of nervous laughter swept across the circle of men.

"I'm going to say it one more time," the man said, "only this time I want you to listen and not laugh." And he said it again: "My shadow mission is to watch TV and masturbate while the world goes to hell."

Silence.

Without an authentic mission, we will be tempted to drift on autopilot, to let our lives center around something that is unworthy, something selfish, something dark— a shadow mission.

Each of us was thinking the same thing: how easily any of our lives can slide into such a self-centered, trivial pursuit. This guy wasn't tempted to be Adolf Hitler or Saddam Hussein. He would have fought against that kind of outright evil. It was the banality of his shadow mission that made it so possible.

I had never heard the phrase before. I had never named what my shadow mission might be. But I understood. I knew.

You and I were created to have a mission in life. We were made to make a difference. But if we do not pursue the mission for which God designed and gifted us, we will find a substitute. We cannot live in the absence of purpose. Without an authentic mission, we will be tempted to drift on autopilot, to let our lives center around something that is unworthy, something selfish, something dark—a shadow mission.

Later on we will learn how to identify and battle both our own shadow missions and the shadow missions of the organizations or teams we lead. But for now I want to underscore just how serious this topic is. When our lives deteriorate into the pursuit of a shadow mission, the world loses. Shadow missions are what we foolishly pursue "while the world goes to hell."

You may scoff at the idea that your shadow mission has any bearing on the larger world. Our eyes remain veiled to the ultimate consequences of our choices. But the Bible tells many stories in which God reveals what the bitter end can be of a shadow mission: death. And the joyous reward of fighting that shadow mission: life. We now turn to one of the classic stories.

Shadow Missions of Epic Proportion

The book of Esther is, among other things, an epic story of missions and shadow missions and how they are woven into the great mission of God. Each character in the story has a choice between a mission and a shadow mission. And as they choose, destinies are formed and the world is changed. We'll look at four characters in particular: King Xerxes, Esther, Haman, and Mordecai.

King Xerxes

Our first character is King Xerxes. His kingdom extended over 127 provinces, from Asia Minor all the way down into Africa, then across to northern parts of India. Although Xerxes was immensely powerful, he was not an admirable character. The writer of Esther uses skill, satire, and exaggeration to give us a picture of an ostentatious king who wants to show off his greatness but in fact has no inner strength of character and constantly needs other people to help him make up his mind.

The story begins with the king at a 180-day banquet—six months of serious partying (three banquets are described in the first chapter alone; one way to divide the book up is as a series of banquets). As the writer puts it, "For a full 180 days [Xerxes] displayed the vast wealth of his kingdom and the splendor and glory of his majesty" (Esther 1:4).

Following that feast, King Xerxes throws another party for the whole capital that is open to common people. The text says, "Wine was served in goblets of gold, each one different from the other, and the royal wine was abundant, in keeping with the king's liberality. By the king's command each guest was allowed to drink with no restrictions, for the king instructed all the wine stewards to serve each man what he wished" (1:7–8). No restrictions, no restraint, unlimited, and everyone drinks from uniquely designed goblets of gold.

On the seventh day, "when King Xerxes was in high spirits from wine" (1:10), he sends for the queen,

Vashti. He has been showing off his possessions; now he wants to show off his ultimate possession, his wife.

What do you think he wants to show them about her? Her brains? "Vashti, darling, why don't you come and entertain my guests by solving some math problems." Her sense of humor? "Vashti, tell us some jokes!" No, he wants Vashti to come "in order to display her beauty to the people and nobles, for she was lovely to look at" (1:11).

Then an extraordinary thing happens. Vashti says no: *Come parade myself before a drunken mob after seven days of Miller time? I don't think so.* She says thanks very much but she would just as soon take a pass and stay home to wash her hair.

You would think the king might realize what an awkward position he put her in, but you'd be wrong. "Then the king became furious and burned with anger" (1:12). Vashti has threatened his shadow mission of impressing a nation. She has made him look weak, and that always provokes a deeply emotional response.

So Xerxes turns to experts in matters of law and justice—their version of the Supreme Court. He can't control the queen, so he makes this a matter of state: "What am I going to do about my wife?" he asks his experts. "I can't do a thing with her. If word gets out about this, then all the wives will rebel against their husbands." Xerxes isn't concerned with justice; he just wants to appear to be in control. He is doing impression management.

Xerxes' supreme court advises him to pass an edict that Vashti not be allowed to come before the king anymore (which probably doesn't break her heart since that is her crime in the first place) and that he get a new queen. As it says in verse 20, "Then when the king's edict is proclaimed throughout all his vast realm, all the women will respect their husbands, from the least to the greatest." Yeah, like that will happen!

Now, part of what's going on here is that the writer is showing us what flatterers these advisers are. They reinforce Xerxes' pride in his "vast and magnificent realm." They all know that the king's shadow mission is ego, appearance, and pleasure. "Make my kingdom about me" could be Xerxes' catchphrase. But these advisers don't name it, they won't challenge it, for the king has surrounded himself with people who will reinforce his shadow mission.

So Xerxes grabs on to their idea. He turns to his "personal attendants" for advice on the search. This is not the Supreme Court; these are his bodyguards, high-testosterone young men who give him their ideas of what to look for in a new queen. Want to guess their number-one criterion? They suggest he hold a "Miss Media and Persia" beauty contest in which each province—127 in all—contributes one finalist to the royal harem. Then each contestant will go through rigorous beauty treatments, the ancient version of extreme makeovers. In the end, the young woman who best pleases the king will become the ultimate trophy wife.

It is hard for us, I know, to believe there was once

a culture so superficial that middle-aged men would try to impress other people by showing they had so much wealth and power that they could attract a wife with youth and beauty. It is hard for us to believe that the human race ever descended to such depths, but once there was such a day.

Esther

One of the contestants is a young Jewish woman named Esther, adopted and raised by her cousin Mordecai. We're told she has a "lovely figure and [is] beautiful" (2:7). She makes it through the prelims and is one of the finalists selected to go before the king.

Think back to the last time you prepared for a big date. I mean when you really wanted to impress your date. How much time did you spend—on hair, face, wardrobe, fragrance? Ever spend just fifteen minutes? Ever spend an hour? Ever spend more time getting ready for the date than you actually spent on the date? Ever have more fun getting ready for the date than you had on the date?

Now look at Esther's date prep time. Not fifteen minutes, not a few hours, not even a day—but a whole year! Before a young woman's turn comes to go in to King Xerxes, she has to complete twelve months of beauty treatments: six months with oil of myrrh, and six months with perfumes and cosmetics (thankfully liposuction and silicone hadn't been invented yet). This is a lot of pressure for a first date. If someone isn't attracted to you after twelve months of prep time, it's probably not going to happen.

Esther, an elegant model of modesty and restraint, wins the contest and is named the new queen. The king throws another party. It looks like Esther's mission is to be arm candy for the most powerful man on earth.

And Esther lives happily ever after, right? Not so much.

Haman

There's another character in this story. His name is Haman, and he is Xerxes' chief of staff. He is a much stronger leader than Xerxes is, but he too has a shadow mission. He is enraged because one man will not bow down and give him worship, and that one man is Mordecai— Esther's cousin and guardian.

Haman is so offended by Mordecai's gall in refusing to bow down to him that Haman goes to King Xerxes and offers him an enormous bribe. It's a huge sum, as much as the amount of money that all of the other countries controlled by Persia at that time would be sending in. All Haman wants is to be allowed to destroy Mordecai and Mordecai's people. And the king's response is basically, "Okay, whatever." He even tells Haman to keep the money. Xerxes doesn't really know which group Haman is ranting about. Because when leaders have been seduced by a shadow mission, they are not likely to challenge anyone else's shadow mission as long as it serves (or doesn't disturb) their own agenda.

Mordecai

When word of Haman's treachery reaches Mordecai, he realizes that there is only one person in the empire in a position to intervene with the king to seek to save all of Israel: the pageant winner. God's plan to save his people is placed in the slender hands of a beauty queen named Esther. And God reveals his mission for Esther through the words of a wise and trusted spiritual friend. "You must go to the king," Mordecai tells her.

Esther doesn't want to do this. She sends word back. Approaching the king unsummoned is a capital offense. And even if he deigns to hold out his gold scepter to her and receive her, he might not be so happy to hear her message that she doesn't like the way he's doing his job. The king is not real open to people defying him publicly. Esther knows what happened to Vashti.

And there is an additional glitch. Esther says, "The king has not summoned me for thirty days." She knows he has a full harem, and he is not a devoted husband. It is

Bible Characters Who Stood Firm Against Their Shadow Mission

Joseph stood firm against the temptations of revenge and sibling rivalry, choosing instead to forgive his brothers and to trust that God would redeem the evil he suffered.

Ruth refused to abandon her mother-in-law even though she could have pursued security and familiarity by returning home. She embraced loyalty and sacrifice over safety and became part of the adventure of redemption.

Daniel repeatedly refused to allow the lure of power to tempt him into compromising his convictions. From what he ate to how he prayed, he chose to honor God, even when it put his ambitions at risk.

Mary, the mother of Jesus. Her great response: "May it be to me according to your word" (Luke 1:38), meant she surrendered all dreams of a normal family life and (as an unwed pregnant woman) her respected reputation.

John the Baptist rejected the temptation of jealousy that his disciples voiced ("Look. [Jesus] is baptizing, and everyone is going to him,") by saying that his destiny and joy were to decrease so that Jesus might increase (John 3:26, 30).

clear to Esther that the king is not as excited about her as he was in earlier days.

At this point many people would back off. But not Mordecai. Mordecai challenges her. "Do not think that because you are in the king's house you alone of all the Jews will escape. For if you remain silent at this time, relief and deliverance for the Jews will arise from another place, but you and your father's family will perish." And he concludes his challenge with these magnificent words, "And who knows but that you have come to royal position for such a time as this?" (4:13–14).

With those few words, Mordecai names the beauty queen's true mission: *Esther, the fate of a whole nation, the fate of God's dream to redeem the world in human terms, at least as far as we can see it right now, rests in your hands. You have not been brought to this point in your life for the sake of accumulating an exquisite wardrobe and precious gems and exotic fragrances; you have not been brought to this point in your life to become the most*

desirable, attractive, applauded woman in the kingdom.
You have not been brought to this point in your life for any
of the reasons that the king thinks you have. You have been
brought to this point to work for justice and to spare your
people a great suffering. You have been brought to this
point to oppose a man who is vile and evil and supremely
powerful. You have a mission, Esther, and your mission
matters. You have been brought to this point in your life not
for yourself, but to be a part of God's plan to redeem the
world. So, Esther, do not let your success at filling society's
shadow mission for women blind you to what God says your
mission really is. Esther, get a clue.

**You have been
brought to this point in
your life not for yourself,
but to be a part of God's plan
to redeem the world.**

Bible Characters Who Succumbed to Their Shadow Mission

Adam and Eve gave in to the original and still most popular shadow mission of all: "You shall be like God."

Solomon, who is supposed to the smartest guy in the world, ends up with a thousand-woman harem.

Judas refused to give Jesus access to that secret, bitter, selfish corner of his heart.

Herod could have been the champion and sponsor of the Messiah, but in his lust for power chose instead to be his rival.

Simon the Sorcerer had a shadow mission to have an impressive ministry. If you look closely, you may still find such shadow missions at work today (Acts 8).

Shadow Mission Revealed

To face a difficult truth without getting discouraged and defensive is one of the great challenges of a leader, and Esther manages to do just that. She tells Mordecai that she wants three days to withdraw with her closest friends for fasting and prayer. Being queen—which she thought was her greatest gift—has become her greatest burden. It is a call for sacrifice, maybe death. She's going to need strength beyond herself for this challenge.

Esther asks Mordecai to gather all of God's people in Susa for three days of fasting and prayer. She refuses to try to achieve this mission based on her beauty and her cleverness and her influence, though they are great. And with words that are as magnificent in their courage as Mordecai's were in their challenge, she declares: "When [the fast] is done, I will go to the king, even though it is against the law. And if I perish, I perish" (4:16). What a heart.

By the way, in a day when writers—even Christian writers—sometimes imply that women are relegated to the sidelines while the real action belongs to the men, it is ironic that one of the great heroes of the Bible is a woman who rejects the stereotype of the beauty queen, who subverts her dim-bulb husband, and who uses all her courage, initiative, and emotional intelligence to resist evil and work for good. So if you are a woman and God has gifted you to lead, for God's sake, for the church's sake, for the sake of this sorry, dark world, *lead*!

If you are a woman and God has gifted you to lead, for God's sake, for the church's sake, for the sake of this sorry, dark world, *lead*!

There were depths in Esther that even she did not suspect—as perhaps there are in you. A few years back there was a (possibly apocryphal) story that somebody at the doll factory messed up, and voice boxes intended for Barbie dolls ended up getting installed in G.I. Joes, and vice versa. Hundreds of kids were shocked to hear G.I. Joe say, "I hope I get asked to the prom!" And an equal number of young girls heard Barbie bark out, "Hit the ground now! Hard, hard, hard!" Xerxes thought he had married Barbie, but he ended up with G.I. Joe.

Impeccable Timing

On the third day, Esther puts on royal robes and stands in the inner court waiting for the king. Heart-pounding, nerve-racking suspense. Imagine what is going through her mind as she waits. *Life or death?*

The king sees Esther. He reaches out his scepter, the indication of royal favor. She will live for another day. He says, "What is it, Queen Esther? What is your request?

Even up to half the kingdom, it will be given you" (5:3).

Esther understands this is the kind of thing a king says when he is in a good mood, but it isn't to be taken literally. If she had actually asked for half the kingdom, things would have changed radically. This was more or less king talk for, "Would you like to hold the remote control tonight?"

Esther couldn't blurt out, "I'd like to have you revoke the unalterable law of the Medes and Persians, spare my people, and put down your chief of staff." So she says, "I'm having a party. You and Haman come."

The king has never turned down a party in his life. So he goes to the party, and they have a great time. And the king says a second time, "Esther, what do you want? Even up to half the kingdom, it's yours."

And Esther says, "If the king regards me with favor and if it pleases the king to grant my petition and fulfill my request"—her verbal skills are remarkable—"let the king and Haman come tomorrow to the banquet I will

prepare for them. Then I will answer the king's question"
(5:8). Esther's negotiating skill here is phenomenal. The
king, by agreeing to attend, has almost already agreed to
her request. Her boldness, her intelligence, and her timing
are breathtaking.

More . . .

We're ready now for the climax of the story, but
the author leaves us in suspense for a moment. He switches
back to Haman. Haman is very excited about what's
going on. Haman is all puffed up in his spirit. He gathers
together his wife and his friends, and he boasts about "his
vast wealth, his many sons, and all the ways the king had
honored him" (5:11). But then he complains, "All this gives
me *no satisfaction* as long as I see that Jew Mordecai
sitting at the king's gate" (5:13, italics added).

Haman has a shadow mission, and I mention this
because many, many people in our culture face this one. It's
maybe the greatest shadow mission of our society, and it's

called "more." More wealth, more power, more applause, more status, more honors—*more*. And Haman goes through his life thinking, *If I can just get more, one day I will have enough.* But it never happens. The Rolling Stones may have recorded the song, but Haman sang it long before them, "I can't get no satisfaction."

Haman's wife advises him to have a gallows built seventy-five feet high and have Mordecai hung on it. Delighted by the suggestion, Haman has the gallows built.

That same night, King Xerxes can't sleep. He asks his servants to read to him (as king, he figures he doesn't have to read himself to sleep) from the annals of the king. "Read that book about *me*," he orders.

And they read to him the story of how a man named Mordecai once saved his life. When the king asks what recognition Mordecai received for his good deed, his servants reply that Mordecai has never been honored. At this moment, Haman arrives to ask the king to hang Mordecai, knowing nothing of the account just read to the king. And the king preempts Haman with a question: "What should be done for the man the king delights to honor?"

Sure that he must be that man, Haman tells the king that the man should be dressed in a royal robe and ride a royal horse led by a royal official and, for good measure, even the horse should wear a crown. "This is what is done," Haman says (nudge, nudge, wink, wink), "for the man the king delights to honor!" (6:9).

Imagine the moment. "Okay," says the king, "the man is Mordecai. Haman, you walk his horse through the city. You tell everybody he's the man I delight to honor."

From here on out it is all downhill for Haman. Esther holds another banquet and engages the king with courage and skill. She tells him that she and her people are to be destroyed.

"Where is he—the man who has dared to do such a thing?" asks the king.

"An adversary and enemy! This vile Haman!" the queen replies.

And Haman ends up being hung on the very gallows he had ordered built for Mordecai.

The king needs a new chief of staff, and Esther arranges that as well, appointing Mordecai over Haman's estate, which the king had given to her. Esther then returns to the king and reminds him that the edict that spelled death for her people is still in effect. The king gives her his ring and says, "Write another decree in the king's name in behalf of the Jews as seems best to you, and seal it with the king's signet ring—for no document written in the king's name and sealed with his ring can be revoked" (8:8).

Noble missions will give rise to noble thoughts, but shadow missions will produce an inner life of hidden darkness and destructive discontent. Shadow missions always destroy at least one person— the one who lives for them.

This new decree gives the Jews the right to defend themselves against Haman's terrorists. And the people of Israel become so feared, we're told, that "many people of other nationalities became Jews" (8:17).

No Accident

This story tells us that our shadow missions have enormous destructive potential. The mission we devote ourselves to will shape us. Our unplanned, involuntary thoughts and wishes will spring out of it. Noble missions will give rise to noble thoughts, but shadow missions will produce an inner life of hidden darkness and destructive discontent. Shadow missions always destroy at least one person—the one who lives for them.

The story of Haman shows us another critical feature of shadow missions. They are almost always slight variations of our authentic missions. This is part of what makes them seductive. Rarely is somebody's shadow mission 180 degrees in the wrong direction. Our shadow missions generally involve the gifts and passions that have been hardwired into us. It's just that we are tempted to misuse them ever so slightly. Our shadow mission leads us just five or ten degrees off our true path in the direction of selfishness or comfort or arrogance. But those few degrees, over time, become the difference between light and shadow.

The story of Esther also suggests that perhaps where you are today is no accident. Who knows but that you have come to your position for such a time as this.

Esther did not set out to be queen, but once she was on the throne, she had to decide between a shadow mission of safety, wealth, and power versus her God-given mission of saving her people.

Haman could have used his position to promote justice, but gave in instead to his shadow mission of self-idolatry and cruelty.

The king could have embraced a mission of generosity, but instead settled for a shadow mission of shallow pleasure.

One thing is certain:
this is your time. Now.
Today. Not some other
situation. Not tomorrow
or yesterday.

What is your position? Don't just think about your
job or your leadership position. You also have influence
through your family, your neighborhood, your volunteer
commitments, and your friendships. One thing is certain:
this is your time. Now. Today. Not some other situation.
Not tomorrow or yesterday. We are often tempted to think
that we are treading water right now, waiting for some
other time, some more important position. You don't get
to choose your time; your time chooses you. You are where
and who you are for a reason.

Jesus' Shadow Mission

Did Jesus face a shadow mission? I think so. We are told by the writer of Hebrews that he, like us, was tempted "in every way"—but was without sin (4:15). For Jesus, the shadow mission was to be a leader without suffering, the Messiah without the cross.

The great New Testament scholar F. F. Bruce writes, "Time and again the temptation came to him from many directions to choose some less costly way of fulfilling that calling than the way of suffering and death, but he resisted it to the end and set his face steadfastly to accomplish the purpose for which he had come into the world."[*]

You remember that in the desert Satan tempts Jesus to achieve his mission without hunger, "Turn these stones to bread. You don't need to be hungry"; without pain, "Throw yourself down from the temple, and the angels will bear you up"; without opposition, "Bow down before me, and all the kingdoms of the earth will be yours."

[*] F. F. Bruce, *The Epistle to the Hebrews, The New International Commentary on the New Testament*, ed. Gordon Fee (Grand Rapids, Mich.: Eerdmans, 1990), 53.

You don't have to be hungry, you don't have to hurt, you don't have to be opposed.

Later on, when Jesus tells the disciples he must suffer and die, Peter tries to convince him that his suffering is unnecessary. This is the same shadow mission, and that is why Jesus rebukes Peter so sharply, saying, "Get behind me, Satan!"

Jesus' shadow mission chased him all the way to the garden of Gethsemane. Again he wrestles with temptation, causing sweat like drops of blood to pour off him. "Oh, Father, let this cup pass from me. Not this."

Even when Jesus is hanging on the cross and people go past him and they're jeering him, what are they doing? It's the same temptation. "Look at him, he saved others, he can't save himself. Why don't you come down if you're the Messiah? There's no such thing as a Messiah that comes with a cross." But Jesus stares the shadow in the face, and at a cost we will never understand, not for all eternity, he says, "No, I will suffer. I will take all of the shadow of the dark, fallen human race on myself. I will go to the cross. I will drink the cup to its last drop." He does that for us. "Not my will, but thine be done."

Without Jesus' sacrifice, without the indwelling of his Spirit, none of us would have the self-knowledge, the courage, or the strength to battle our own shadow missions. We would be as self-absorbed as Xerxes, as unsatisfied and power hungry as Haman. We would be a mere shadow of the selves God intended us to be.

Giftedness and Character

The battle between mission and shadow mission points to a fundamental distinction between two aspects of our makeup. There is a crucial difference between *giftedness* and *character.*

By *giftedness* I mean talents and strengths: high IQ, athletic ability, charm, business savvy, leadership skills, charisma, good looks, popularity, artistic talent. These gifts are very good things. They all come from God. The Bible says that he is the giver of "every good and perfect gift" (James 1:17), and that we should be grateful when such gifts come our way.

But your gifts are not the most important thing about you. There is something else you have that is called *character*. Character is your moral and spiritual makeup; it is your habitual tendencies, the way you think and feel and intend and choose. The makeup of what is called character is what makes people trustworthy or undependable, humble or arrogant. It's a word that sounds old-fashioned—kind of Victorian—but it is not. It is who we are at the absolute core of our personhood.

Character determines our capacity to be with God, to experience God, and to know God. It determines our ability to love and relate to other people. All that is part of our character. When we are called to imitate Jesus—to be "imitators of Jesus"—we are not being called to have his giftedness or his role. Rather, we are striving for his character.

You can't envy good character. There's something about a Christlike character that is so good that even the desiring of it cannot harm us.

Giftedness is good, but it's not the greatest good. It's important to be clear on this because we live in a culture that idolizes giftedness. This is the way, in our culture, that we get the "stuff" our culture tells us we ought to want. Giftedness is the path to the good stuff. Giftedness is what makes other people look at you and say, "Wow!" It puts people on magazine covers. Therefore, we are tempted to put more energy into wanting and enhancing our giftedness than paying attention to what is going on in our character and just slowing down and asking God to reform our character.

When we idolize giftedness, we often end up envying other people's giftedness. I see someone else who is more gifted than I am in some area, and I wish that I had their gift, or I wish that they didn't have it. Their giftedness kind of sticks in my craw.

The desire for good character, however, never leads to envy. You can't envy good character. There's something about a Christlike character that is so good that even the desiring of it cannot harm us.

People who are highly gifted can use those gifts to pursue their mission or their shadow mission. People with well-formed characters recognize that their shadow mission is unworthy and undesirable.

In the absence of good character, the giftedness of people will not be used well. The more gifted we are, the more arrogant and self-centered and destructive we are apt to be. Lavish giftedness in the absence of well-formed character will always lead us toward our shadow mission.

Samson: Crushed by Giftedness

There is a man in Scripture who is very gifted, but who doesn't have the character to bear his giftedness. Giftedness always comes at a price: pressures, temptations, a sense of entitlement. Without character, your giftedness will crush you. As it did Samson.

We read in the book of Judges, chapter 13, about how an angel of God comes to a childless couple and tells them they are going to have a son. He tells them God will gift their son lavishly, and the son must devote himself to God. He will be a powerful leader. He will deliver his people from living under the heel of the Philistines.

Their son, Samson, is to be a "Nazirite." This designation is an obscure idea taken from Numbers, the fourth book in the Old Testament, in which God says that if people want to devote themselves to him in a special way, they can enter into a season of commitment and devotion—a time when they take three vows to remind themselves of their commitment. First, they will touch no dead body. Second, they will drink no wine. And third, they will not cut their hair. There is nothing particularly virtuous about any of these promises. They are just temporary vows, but they are symbols, concrete reminders, that someone is devoted to do something for God. For Samson, these vows are to be a way of life. They are to help Samson cultivate a strong sense of his devotion to God. There will be certain options in his life that he needs to say no to, and vow-keeping will give him the inner strength to do so.

Samson grows up, a man of extraordinary gifts. He lives in a culture where physical strength matters, and he has it in spades. He can take a wild animal apart with his bare hands. He can defeat a dozen normal men in hand-to-hand combat. He is such a dazzling specimen that men want to be him, and women want to be with him. He has charisma, that kind of magnetism that makes people want to follow him into battle and adventure and into the unknown. He has power. He is what was called at that time in Israel a "judge."

Samson "da Man"

At that time, Israel did not have kings. Judges were the leaders of all the people. They were not like judges in our day where a person sits on a bench and tries cases. A judge in this time was the supreme political and military authority over all of Israel. Samson was the big dog, the alpha male. People would come up to him and say, "You da man, Samson." Samson would not say, "No, no, no. You da man." Samson would say, "You're right. I am da man."

I have tried to think of who he would be like in our day. He would be like a champion body builder with an incredible physique, but have the glamour of a movie star who could headline big-budget action flicks and maybe use that glamour to go into politics and become "Governator" of his entire state—that kind of a figure. Then add to all of that the fact that he had spiritual anointing. He was used by God.

One of the intriguing parts of his story is that sometimes God uses Samson *because of* what he does.

And sometimes God uses Samson *in spite of* what he does. Samson's story shows us that even when there is spiritual anointing, even where there is impressive ministry, giftedness never makes up for a lack of character.

Samson, in quick succession, breaks two of the three Nazirite vows: he touches a dead body (the carcass of a lion he killed) in order to eat the honey inside. Because he never learned to say no to his appetite, he breaks his vow to God. Later, at a bachelor party he throws for himself, he drinks wine, breaking vow number two (Judges 14). But it's the breaking of the final vow that is the most famous—and most tragic.

The Has-been Strong Guy

Samson falls in love with Delilah, a Philistine woman. Her being a Philistine is bad enough; the Philistines are about as far away from Israel's values and culture as they can be. They worship a god they call "Baal-Zebub" (2 Kings 1:2), Lord Baal. Their religion is so evil that cultic prostitution is an important part of worship of Lord Baal, as is infant sacrifice. This is so repulsive to the Hebrews that, as a term of derision, they call the Philistine god "Beelzebub." Does that sound familiar? *Beelzebub* is Hebrew for "Lord of the Flies." Beelzebub is a dark god associated with the place where flies gather—on a dung heap.

The Philistines begin to use Delilah to get to Samson—to find out the secret of his physical strength.

Delilah keeps asking Samson, "What's the secret to your strength?" He keeps making up answers. Finally she says to him, "How can you say, 'I love you,' when you won't confide in me? This is the third time you have made a fool of me and haven't told me the secret of your great strength" (Judges 16:15).

She continues to pester Samson until he is sick to death of it and tells her everything. This big, strong man—this charismatic, magnetic leader—tells a nagging woman everything. "No razor has ever been used on my head," he says, "because I have been a Nazirite dedicated to God from my mother's womb. If my head were shaved, my strength would leave me, and I would become as weak as any other man" (Judges 16:17).

And now you understand the significance of the hair. This is the one vow Samson has never broken, and now, because he's hooked up with the wrong partner, because he never learned to say no to his appetites, because he never learned to tolerate frustration and disappointment, this man who was given such lavish gifts shreds the final vestige of his devotion to God and breaks the last vow. Now he is no longer a Nazirite; he's just a has-been strong guy.

You know the rest of this story. He goes to sleep. Delilah cuts off his hair and ties him up. When the Philistines come to take him away, Samson jumps up and thinks he will fight them. Then comes one of the saddest statements in the Bible: "But he did not know that the LORD had left him" (Judges 16:20).

He did not know.

Character is, among other things, the capacity to be inhabited by God. Every wrong choice, every dark thought I entertain, makes me a little less sensitive to the Divine presence. In the end, Samson's character was so eroded that he didn't sense its erosion or realize how absent God was from his life. The success of giftedness can mask the erosion of character. Samson did not have the character to bear his giftedness. In the end, the Philistines captured him and gouged out his eyes.

If you don't develop the character to support your gifts, they will actually become destructive to you.

Ironically, it was not until Samson had lost his vision—not until he was blind, humiliated, and imprisoned—that he called out to God for help. But even in death his story is ambiguous. He asks for strength from God to "get revenge on the Philistines for my two eyes" (Judges 16:28). His life ends, as it was lived, in the ambiguity of the shadow: great power, a desire to serve God, mixed with a desire for vengeance.

Character Formation

Like Samson, you might be extraordinarily gifted. But if you don't develop the character to support your gifts, they will actually become destructive to you. Your shadow mission will win out and your gifts will crush you. It's only a matter of time.

You don't have a choice about what gifts you're given. But you *are* given a choice of what character you will build. Character—having the ability to grow in the character of Jesus—is available to anyone who wants it.

But we don't live in a culture that exalts character. The challenge about Christlike character formation is that it's time-consuming, it's not very glamorous, and it won't get you very much at all . . . except life with God . . . except the healing of your broken, hungry, wounded, hurting, tired heart . . . except the satisfaction of your soul . . . things that giftedness can never achieve.

To say it again: character formation is absolutely fundamental to our well-being, but it's not glamorous. So often—in our work, in our lives, even in our churches—we think, "Man, there's so much going on, we can't take the time to work on 'character.'" The question really is: Who do we want to be? We can do really impressive-looking things, but what we take into eternity is *who we become*.

So how do we go about doing this nebulous thing called "building character"? Well, character-building has one of those odd dynamics where you generally cannot pursue it directly. Somebody might say, "I'm gonna try really hard to be humble today." But trying really hard

> We can do really impressive-looking things, but what we take into eternity is *who we become.*

doesn't create humility. And if you manage to feel humble for a moment, your next thought is, *Wow, I'm being so humble, how come other people can't be more like this?*

When it comes to character formation, you need to use the principle of indirection. It's a bit like happiness. Joy, of course, is part of a healthy character, but you cannot pursue happiness by making it the primary focus of your life. Joy comes as a by-product of the pursuit of other things. And I believe that character comes as a by-product of the pursuit of God and the kingdom of God.

We cannot do character-building through moral self-improvement. The redeeming of our characters is a God-size job. But we are not passive. There are practices we can engage in that can help in character formation. Richard Foster wrote very wisely about this in his classic book *The Celebration of Discipline*. He identifies a number of practices that, when pursued wisely and with serious intent, can help lead to spiritual growth. So if, for instance, humility is something I really need to work on, I might engage in acts of service. Or if I use language to intimidate or exaggerate or deceive, then the practice of silence will be very important for me.

The idea of pursuing spiritual practices or disciplines can sound intimidating. In general, "discipline" is not a happy term in our day. But it's important to remember that these practices are all simply a means to an end. Anyone who is hungry for change in any area of life will pursue them. We think of ascetics back in the Middle Ages as being strange people. But many of the greatest ascetics of our day are playing in the NFL or performing in concert halls. They put their bodies through serious and wise training to be able to do what they deeply desire to do: sack quarterbacks or play "Stairway to Heaven."

Often in our day people think of training simply as something they do to develop their giftedness. But wise people have always understood that development of character also requires "training." We do this by asking what good character looks like. We ask, *What are the obstacles that keep me from having that kind of character? Am I prone to gossip, or laziness, or bitterness, or selfishness, or power, or apathy?* Then we ask, *What are the practices*

We cannot do character-building through moral self-improvement. The redeeming of our characters is a God-size job. But we are not passive.

through which I might receive power to live a different kind of life? Always, the goal of disciplines is freedom. I want to be free to do the right thing at the right time in the right way for the right reason.

One of the classic examples of shadow mission in our day is the problem of addiction. We have a friend named Sheila—tall, articulate, charismatic, bright—an Ivy-League lawyer. But her shadow mission was to feel good. And eventually her shadow mission caused her to drink as much as possible as often as possible to avoid as much pain as possible. For a long time her giftedness got a lot of people to make a lot of excuses for her. But eventually she was told that one more bender would mean the loss of her job.

She bent. Again.

She ended up in the rehab ward of a psychiatric hospital. Her doctor told her to go to an AA meeting the first morning. She said, "I'm not going to go to a meeting with a bunch of drunks at 6:00 a.m." He replied, "Not only are you going, you're going to fix coffee for a bunch of drunks at 6:00 a.m."

She went. She fixed coffee. She joined the club. She began to follow the Twelve Steps. And through these practices—surrender, self-examination, confession, accountability, and so on—she began to receive the power to do what she could not do on her own. She received freedom from her shadow mission. One day at a time.

Find Your Mordecai

Character-building rarely happens in isolation. We'll never successfully battle our shadow mission if we don't have someone who will speak truth to us. Everyone needs a Mordecai.

What do I mean? Think back to the story of Esther. Do you think Esther would have given up her shadow mission of a life of ease and relaxing beauty regimens without the stirring challenge of Mordecai? Doubtful. Would she have realized the danger she was in? Doubtful. Would she have acted on it? Even more doubtful. Only from her trusted guardian Mordecai was she able to hear

Who loves you
enough to challenge you
when you're ready to settle
for your shadow mission?

and accept a challenge, even when all her self-protective
instincts told her to say no. Esther and Samson were
perhaps the epitome of stereotypically gifted femininity
and masculinity of their day. One of the biggest differences
between them is that Esther had a Mordecai, and Samson
did not.

Who is the Mordecai in your life? Who loves
you enough to challenge you when you're ready to
settle for your shadow mission? If you're part of an elder
board or a leadership team, whether it's at your church
or your workplace, do you have regular, honest, fearless

conversations about the reality of your shadow mission? If you are in the leadership position on that team, do you model this, do you initiate it? If you are a leader and you do not know your shadow mission, I guarantee that you're the only one on your leadership team who does not know your shadow mission. Everybody else knows it, and they talk about it.

So find your Mordecai. A Mordecai is someone who is more devoted to the development of your character than impressed by your giftedness. Often this person is a spouse or close friend. But even those closest to you don't always see every aspect of your life. You'll need other family members or friends or colleagues who love you, people you can trust, people who can speak truth to you. Ask them to tell you when you're going down the wrong road. Then listen to them.

Name Your Shadow Mission

Up until now, I've been putting off the topic of identifying your shadow mission. First, I wanted you to understand the life-or-death consequences of shadow missions. And then I wanted you to be clear about how important character is in fighting your shadow mission, and how giftedness can sometimes blind us to the need for character. But now's the time to tackle it, because in order to fight your shadow mission you need to name your shadow mission. You can't fight the enemy if it doesn't have a name.

I've been through lots of exercises on developing a personal mission statement, and to tell you the truth, I've had a hard time coming up with a mission statement that sticks. I can identify the general areas about which I'm passionate, but coming up with a snappy, memorable, meaningful phrase—a catchphrase—has been difficult.

Not so with my shadow mission. I've known it since I was twelve years old, and I can sum it up in four words. I used to do some speaking when I was a little kid in our hometown. A newspaper reporter covered one of those occasions. The headline for the story was "Talkative boy wins acclaim." That's my shadow mission catchphrase. I know that, apart from God's help, my life would be an exercise in self-idolatry, a fruitless effort to win approval. I fight this shadow mission every day, and I will fight it the rest of my life. People I love get hurt by it.

I think of a man I talked to a while ago, a business leader in the corporate world. He was married with small children, and his family complained that he was never home. To this he said, "They don't understand; I'm doing it all for them."

"Really?" I challenged him. "Is it really true that you are doing it all for them? Why are you doing it for them when they don't want you to be doing it? If they did not exist, would your life look a lot different than it does now? Would you not be working the same way that you are?"

In reality, he was not doing it for them. It was clear who he was doing it for. In fact, his catchphrase could have been the exact opposite of what he'd said, namely: "They do understand; I'm doing it all for me!"

I think of a woman I know who was head of a faith-based educational organization. Smart as a whip. Tons of energy. Lots of drive. But her single most commonly used phrase was, "I'm sorry." Not "Let's take the hill." Not "We're lucky to be doing this." Not "Let's charge into tomorrow."

"I'm sorry."

And the dirty little secret, the truth behind all her apologies that no one knew—not even she knew—was that she wasn't sorry. She was afraid. And if you could have poked way down underneath the fear, I think you would have found some anger glowering around. I think she was mad at other people for not liking her when she was always so nice, and mad at herself for saying "sorry" so often when she wasn't.

For she had a shadow mission, though it was subtle. Her shadow mission was to be liked. Or to so out-nice everybody that if they didn't like her she could feel justified in judging them or dismissing their criticisms. Her shadow mission was so bathed in apologies that it almost looked radiant. But it was a shadow mission all the same. At the core it wasn't "nice" at all. It was all about avoiding conflict and evading unpleasantness and escaping criticism. It was, as all shadow missions are, truth-resistant. In the end, it sucked all the integrity and life out of her, and she left her calling. On her way out, in her farewell address to the troops, she said, "I'm sorry."

Just think of how much heartache could have been prevented if people were alerted to their shadow missions. That's why it's so important for you to seek out your shadow mission—so you can destroy it.

Before you try to name your shadow mission, however, it's a good idea to sit quietly for a while. Pray. Ask the Holy Spirit to open your eyes, for God promises to give wisdom to those who ask for it (James 1:5). Paul uses the image of a suit of armor because this kind of work is a battle—it requires the belt of truth, the breastplate of righteousness (character again!), the shield of faith (you can't do this on your own), the helmet of salvation (we don't even ride bikes without helmets anymore, and this is a lot more dangerous), and the sword of the Spirit (Ephesians 6:10–18; Hebrews 4:11–13).

Think back on the past. Ask: When have I failed? When have I felt shame? When has a gentle whisper indicated I've gone off track?

Read the list of "Top Ten Shadow Missions" (page 65). Recognize any of them from firsthand experience? Or did you see your own shadow mission reflected in the stories of Esther or Samson or some other Bible character?

Write down your reflections, if you're the writing type. Circle your temptations. Zero in on your failings. Then try to boil it all down to a sentence, then a catchphrase, maybe a single word. Run it past your "Mordecai" to see if someone who knows you well sees this in you.

Top Ten Shadow Missions

1. Just give me home, health, and a hefty 401(k).

2. Busy, busy, busy.

3. I don't care who's in charge—as long as it's me.

4. Show me the money.

5. It *is* all about me.

6. Maintaining hidden addictions.

7. I'll think about it tomorrow.

8. Looking nice by avoiding conflict.

9. Climb the ladder first, put people second.

10. Shop till you drop.

A friend of mine went through this exercise. After some thought and prayer, here is how she summarized her shadow mission:

Sentence: I fall into living my shadow mission when I get so busy that accomplishing tasks becomes more important to me than loving God and my neighbor.

Catchphrase: To-do list all done.

One word: Busyness.

You may find that you battle multiple shadow missions. Their names are legion! For now, however, choose to focus on just one: the one you most want to hide. Work on that one for a while. There will be plenty of time to get around to number two. (Unless your number one is procrastination.) You really can trust that God will lead you in the process.

Finally, if, after all this, you still can't name your shadow mission, get outside help. Find your Mordecais and ask them!

Focus on Joy

Now that you've done all that heavy lifting in agonizing reflection and self-evaluation, it's time to take a break. Literally. One of the best ways to battle your shadow mission is by not focusing on it at all. Instead focus on joy. Non-strategic joy.

Strategic joy is the joy that comes from successfully executing a plan. As such, it often is tied in to a shadow mission.

Non-strategic joy has nothing to do with a person's success or ability or power. It just *is*.

One of the best
ways to battle your shadow
mission is by not focusing on
it at all. Instead focus on joy.
Non-strategic joy.

Spending time with non-strategic people is a great source of pure joy. Wrestling with your kids on the floor. Mentoring that schoolchild in your community. Hanging out with your friends. Going on a date with your husband or wife. All of those things are incredibly helpful in providing non-strategic joy.

For me, over the last year or so, a non-strategic source of joy has been golf. Now golf can be pretty close to a shadow mission in and of itself. I started playing it and I liked doing it. But golf doesn't help me achieve any goals or do anything important; to me it's just pure joy. And if I work out a little frustration by imagining someone's face on that tiny white ball as I hit it, all the better!

God gave us another amazing source of non-strategic joy: worship. Whether it's with a pipe organ or a praise team, with liturgy or laughing in the Spirit, pure unadulterated worship of God is the very best antidote to the shadow mission that darkens our hearts. Worship is (or should be) pure joy. Indulge in it regularly.

Shadow Missions in Organizations

As my eyes have been opened to the idea of shadow missions, I've seen that they don't just afflict leaders. They also infect whole organizations.

The church I serve is just a couple of miles away from prestigious Stanford University in the heart of Silicon Valley. If Babel were built in the twenty-first century, this area probably would bid on the project. Venture capitalists and sleep-on-the-cot entrepreneurs and million-dollar fixer-upper houses and alpha techies live together in the land of billionaire dreams. Highly educated, highly affluent, highly overworked. The next community over is East Palo Alto, which, a few years ago, led the nation in murders per capita. But it is a world away.

The staff named the church's shadow mission years before I ever got there, just by nature of the location. They didn't use the phrase "shadow mission," but that's what they were describing. They sometimes joked that the motto of the church should be: "A successful church for successful people."

Just imagine if your church's shadow mission was posted on the sign out front or printed on its stationery. What might your telling catchphrase be? "We may not be growing, but we'll judge churches that are." "Successfully avoiding conflicts since 1893." "We take care of our own—and you're not one of us."

Businesses and nonprofits are not immune to acquired mission deficiency syndrome either. An accounting firm starts with a mission of giving honest feedback and financial practices to businesses—to help create accountability. But after a time the firm gets larger, draws more clients, and the mission shifts to "maintaining and increasing our bigness without getting caught at doing anything illegal." After a while, the "without getting caught" of that shadow mission decreases in importance. From that moment on the clock is ticking.

A corporation is born with a dream to provide

energy for people that is inexpensive and good for the environment. Profits go up. Then the pressure becomes to increase the profits, even though it's at the expense of the original vision. The people at the top are described as giants by leading publications in their field. Eventually the mission becomes: "Maintain the vast egos of the people at the top." Mergers and kickbacks and dubious quarterly reporting strategies and lavish offices and bloated top-level financial practices all exist just out of public view; they are generally known inside the company. These strategies are indicators of the corporation's shadow mission.

An elected government official is so powerful that he engineers the downfall of numerous rivals, making it possible for him to virtually handpick the person against whom he will run. He keeps a list of his enemies. He encourages a culture in which those who report to him are ruthless in their arrogance and power. Eventually, whatever mission was present at the start is overtaken by the shadow mission, and the whole house of cards tumbles down.

A hi-tech corporation is so committed to opening up foreign markets that it allows its technology to be used by a totalitarian government to acquire information on political dissidents, who are then imprisoned unjustly. When this is made public, the hi-tech corporation's executives shrug their shoulders. Ethical scruples would be preferred, but must not be allowed to interfere with the shadow mission of global dominance.

A CEO hires detectives to spy on her staff and board because the shadow mission has become "Compliance and loyalty at all costs."

Heads of companies and real estate tycoons use books and seminars and TV shows to turn their faces and names into a brand, serving the shadow mission that declares: "Being the ultimate winner is everything."

Leading Your Team Into Battle

As the preceding examples reveal, identifying and battling your own shadow mission is good, but any good leader will also identify and battle the shadow mission of the company or church or organization that he or she leads. And the best way to do that is to alert the whole team to the concept of shadow missions, so that together you all know the face of the enemy you are battling.

Call a Retreat

If you lead a team, you may want to use some extended meetings or even a retreat to introduce and then probe the topic of shadow mission. It may be helpful for you to go off-site to give your team members distance from their day-to-day tasks so they can focus instead on these larger issues. And as with any retreat, be sure to include some fun to lighten up the mood and to encourage relationship building.

Depending on the existing team atmosphere and the relationships among your team members, this topic of shadow mission either has the potential to be intriguing and energizing or intimidating and threatening.

It helps for people to know that every human being and every organization wrestles with this. The question isn't *if* you have a shadow mission, it's if you'll deal with it. You may want to talk about the examples of some individuals or churches or companies or administrations that you have seen crippled by the shadow mission dynamic. Understanding what's at stake can help fuel people's energy for this discussion.

As a leader, you will be served by understanding a simple truth: Everybody who reports to you already understands your shadow mission—probably better than you do. A century ago a great scholar by the name of W. E. B. DuBois noted that African Americans had a great gift to give to white America—if white America would only accept it. It is the gift he called "double vision"—the ability to see

The question isn't
if you have a
shadow mission,
it's if you'll
deal with it.

the country from both the inside and the outside—because

his people had been held outside by those with power

inside. The shadow mission of those in power is seen most

clearly by those who are under that power. So as a leader,

if you're afraid to reveal the truth that you have a shadow

mission to those who report to you, relax. They already

know. They probably know your shadow mission better than

you do.

When you sense that you and your team are ready

to deal with this issue, begin your meeting, if you can, with

a time of prayer. Give some thought to what the prayer will

look like. You may want to spend some time in confession. Give people a chance to be honest before God about their own shadow sides. Then spend some time in prayer asking for grace. Take the time to receive forgiveness and mercy from God. Ask for illumination and wisdom. We are never able to see the whole truth about ourselves without God's help. Encourage people to ask God for wisdom about how to speak hard words with both truth and love.

Then introduce the idea of shadow mission. Define it, explore it. You may want to hand out a copy of this book to each of your team members and have them spend time alone reading it and thinking about their own shadow mission. Discuss the general idea of shadow mission, but don't put anyone on the spot or ask anyone to name their own shadow mission unless they feel absolutely comfortable doing so.

You might think that publicly identifying one's own shadow mission may be more accepted or needed in a church setting than in a business setting, since in a church setting we are called to be spiritually accountable to each other. But I don't think this is the case. Patrick Lencioni, author of numerous bestsellers on leadership, writes that at the foundation of a healthy team is trust, and what is core to building trust is the appropriate vulnerability of a leader. True vulnerability can never be faked. It always comes with a little risk, a little pain.

Name Your Organization's Shadow Mission

Once you sense that everyone understands the concept of shadow mission, spend time as a team identifying or naming your organization's shadow mission. You might want to start by making a list of times when your team has gotten off track. That varies from team to team. For some teams it might be lack of structure or inability to take things seriously; for others it might be focusing on the wrong issues. You might want to identify the indicators or warning lights that signal that a shadow operation is at work. Spend some time listing possible

> How do you know
> when you've named your
> shadow mission? How do you
> know when you've put your finge
> on it? It's like the roar of a lion
> in the jungle; when you hear it,
> you *just know.*

shadow missions in sentence form, catchphrase form, and as a single word.

How do you know when you've named your shadow mission? How do you know when you've put your finger on it? It's like the roar of a lion in the jungle; when you hear it, you *just know.* When it's named, there will be this little release of energy, maybe laughter, maybe embarrassment, certainly recognition. People on the team will say, "That's it! That's us!" One of the reasons we laugh at and remember catchphrases like "Successfully avoiding conflict since 1973" is that flash of recognition, an aha moment of "I'm like that" or "I know someone who's just like that." That's the moment you want to focus on with your discussion.

Finally, you may want to find a Mordecai—someone outside the organization who can address shadow mission issues with the whole team. Someone from the outside often can see things that people on the inside can't see. My wife is my greatest encourager and friend, and she is also my most effective Mordecai. I recently spoke at an event during the first week of January, and someone afterward said, a little hyperbolically, "That was the highlight of my year." My wife was standing next to me. Her immediate response was, "The year is young yet."

Form a Battle Strategy

Once you identify your team's shadow mission, spend time forming a battle strategy. List ways you can combat that shadow mission. Is there an accountability structure that needs to be formed? Is there a system or

Top Ten Shadow Missions for Organizations

1. Success for the sake of success.

2. A fearless squadron of yes-men.

3. Why risk walking on water when we can tread it?

4. People are made to be used.

5. Maintain the system.

6. Stay out of my silo.

7. It's all about politics.

8. Mastering the art of malicious compliance.

9. Cynicism R Us.

10. Avoiding accountability.

> Probably the single
> most important tool in
> battling the shadow
> mission is solitude. Solitude
> is critical to the formation
> of human character.

schedule or routine that needs to be changed? Is there a

way you can keep that shadow mission in the forefront

of the team's consciousness, a gentle or humorous way to

remind your team of the shadow mission without becoming

heavy-handed, negative, or annoying about it?

Probably the single most important tool in

battling the shadow mission is solitude. Solitude is critical

to the formation of human character. I find it striking that

it was in solitude where Jesus came most excruciatingly

face-to-face with his own shadow mission. It was during

the forty days in the desert when the Evil One tempted

him to be a messiah without hunger, without pain, without

opposition. And it was in solitude that Jesus battled his shadow mission and was given the grace to say no.

As a leader, I need to regularly withdraw from the people and conversations and systems that normally surround me because even when they are filled with good intentions and constructive activities, over time I will be tempted to use them for the pursuit of my shadow mission. It is when I am alone that the shadow is unmasked. It is when I am alone that I remember no mission on earth can give me what I want most—which is to be loved and valued by my heavenly Father.

One of the purposes of tragedy is to knock us off our high horse, to help us humbly recognize our capacity for giving in to the shadow.

And what is true for me is true as well for the people who serve with me, who serve above me, who serve under me. We must withdraw from each other so that we are free of the need to impress or dominate or use each other. Then we are able to name our shadow missions to one another, to laugh about them, confess them, point out when they are reemerging, and call each other to a deeper mission.

It is also helpful to review our goals. What do we measure? If our shadow mission as an organization is "Be big," then we had better measure something other than just attendance. For instance, we could measure the number of times per year those of us in leadership serve food in a homeless shelter, or consistently volunteer our time in other ways.

I'll give you another tool that may surprise you: read great literature. I know that to activist leaders, such reading can seem like a waste of time. But tragedies like *Macbeth* or *Hamlet* or *King Lear* are stories of shadow missions. Greek philosopher Aristotle said that one of the essential ingredients for an effective tragedy is that we must be able to identify with the central character. One of the purposes of tragedy is to knock us off our high horse, to help us humbly recognize our capacity for giving in to the shadow. However, as author Alain de Botton points out, the tone of modern culture and tabloid journalism often panders to the opposite emotion: how could those strange, pathetic celebrities/politicians/CEOs have such unthinkable flaws? He notes that if *Othello* were a modern-day story, the newspaper headlines would be something like "Love-Crazed Immigrant Kills Senator's Daughter." Or Oedipus, the king, might get "Royalty Caught in Incest Shocker."[*] The very act of leadership can reinforce our illusions of pride and omnicompetence. We read to understand that we all carry a Haman or a Samson or a Macbeth or an Othello inside our hearts.

---

[*] Alain de Botton, *Status Anxiety* (New York: Pantheon, 2004), 149ff.

Restore the Strays Gently

Finally, as team leader, you need to be a sort of shepherd, looking out for team members who stray off track into their shadow missions, gently leading them back into the fold. Often when someone gets off track we tend to ignore the behavior, not wanting to make waves, or we tend to excuse it or rationalize it, especially if the person is a star performer. If we're removed from those who are straying, we may gossip about them or judge them. But none of those responses is helpful and, in the long run, they're positively harmful.

In Galatians 6:1, Paul says, "If someone is caught in a sin, you who live by the Spirit should restore that person gently." The operative word is *restore*. Restoration takes time; it takes wisdom; it takes thoughtfulness and gentle care. Even those in the business world have occasion to take disciplinary action. As Jesus pointed out, on those occasions the first step is to talk with the person face-to-face in private (Matthew 18:15).

Here's an example of someone doing that for me. About a month ago, I was talking with a close friend about a conversation I had with my wife, in which Nancy told me she felt I was being less than helpful around the house. I mentioned that my shadow mission at home tends to be self-preoccupation and passivity. And this friend said, "You know what, I see that in you. I have found myself lately thinking sometimes I want to talk with you or email you, but I hold back because I feel like I will be an interruption to you."

This friend didn't make any accusations. In fact, he wasn't charging me with anything. He was merely commenting on what he found going on inside of him as he related to me. He's somebody I'm quite close to, and it was painful to think that someone I care about could feel like he was an interruption. We had a long talk about it, and later I reflected on this quite a bit. I realized that when I go into shadow mission mode, I use my energy and giftedness

> When I go into shadow
> mission mode, I use my energy
> and giftedness to get people to
> applaud me, and the people
> close to me feel like I don't
> have time for them.

to get people to applaud me, and the people close to me
feel like I don't have time for them. It was a humbling
realization.

Whether you are battling an individual or a
corporate shadow mission, some of the symptoms of the
disease and strategies to fight it will be the same. For your
convenience, I've summarized them in two sidebars (pages
88–90). Use these sidebars to jumpstart your own diagnosis
and to form your battle strategy.

Symptoms of a
Shadow Mission in Action

- **A chronic sense of soul dissatisfaction.** At work I feel less like a human being and more like a cog in a machine.

- **Emotional indicators.** Irritability, lack of gratitude or joy, deep impatience, a sense of stagnation. Difficulty in achieving or maintaining motivation. When I slow down, I wonder: "Why am I doing this?"

- **A sense of smugness, exclusiveness, and self-congratulatory pride.** I have a constant need to pump myself up by contrasting our organization with other organizations in our field that are less impressive.

- **Busyness at unimportant tasks.** I have lost a sense of meaning in what I do. I default to rote compliance rather than genuine engagement.

- **Relationships are superficial.** People become objects to use. Anonymity is pervasive. People do not know each other outside the cubicle. Supervisors do not care about the lives and families and interests of those they supervise. Few friendships happen at work. People feel unknown.

- **Self-aggrandizement.** My gifts are used not to glorify God, but to gratify myself.

- **Lack of authenticity.** Leaders give motivational speeches, but the tone feels hyped up, contrived, manipulative. Missing are simple, sincere descriptions of why what we do matters. People give surface responses, but underneath is widespread complaining and withdrawal, expressed covertly and destructively.

- **Running on empty.** There is a sense among the staff that the organization is spending down the relational reserves that were built up in earlier, healthier, more devoted days.

- **Loss of excellence.** It is no longer clear to people what it looks like to be effective. What was once a clear and compelling vision is increasingly replaced by "complaint management" or "survival" behaviors.

Strategies for Battling Your Shadow Mission

- **Spend time in solitude and silence.** Make time for solitude—for yourself and for other members of the team—so you can come to clarity about what your shadow mission is.

- **Be humbly open to truth.** Read great literature with a repentant spirit.

- **Be honest.** Name your shadow mission with courage, precision, and humor.

- **Identify the consequences.** Reflect together how destructive it would be to give in to the organization's shadow mission and recommit to fight it.

- **Quantify progress.** Decide how to measure and clearly gauge movement away from the shadow mission.

- **Celebrate.** As a team, regularly celebrate progress in moving toward your organization's true mission.

From Shadow Mission to the One Vision that Matters

While it's important to build your character and identify your shadow mission, in truth you need only one thing. Without this one thing you can name your shadow mission and claim it and battle it—and still lose. That one essential thing is a vision of God and the reality of his kingdom.

The Reformation. The Great Awakening. The Jesus People Movement. As Dallas Willard points out in his fabulous little booklet *Living in the Vision of God*, any great movement of God begins with a vision. That vision is not about what the person or church or movement is going to do. It's not even a vision about the future.

The vision that really matters is the vision of how good God is and how blessed I am to be his child. This vision, of an already existing reality, sees the goodness and competence of God. Then out of the goodness of that vision grows a desire to do something for God, to make his kingdom real. Because God's work is all-comprehensive, the need for this vision is as great for business or for schools as it is for local churches. All human work is meant to be rooted in what God is doing.

Over time, as a movement or organization or church grows, people start to focus on what's growing rather than on the reality of God. And then the shadow mission replaces the kingdom of God vision. Once that happens, it's just a matter of time before everything falls apart. Questions like these get in the way: How do we make this thing bigger? How do we make it better? How do we at

Over time, as a movement or organization or church grows, people start to focus on what's growing rather than on the reality of God. And then the shadow mission replaces the kingdom of God vision.

least keep it propped up? And we become preoccupied with numbers, goals, and programs, and people live with stress, exhaustion, fatigue, and competition. Before we know it, we've not only lost the essential God vision but we've lost our true mission and slid into shadow mission.

The only safe way to lead a team is to be rooted in this God vision. It's not a vision of what might happen someday. It's a vision of what already *is*. It's a vision of God and the goodness of God. If I can live in that vision, then I will seek to do good things with God, and I won't be clutching onto outcomes in a life-or-death manner.

When I first arrived at the church I serve, I realized what a mistake it is to begin: "Okay, here's where we're going. Here's where I'm going to lead you." Instead, we had to learn together to start with the reality of God. With what a good God we worship. With living in the freedom and joy of God's presence.

I also realized I could not lead people I did not know and who did not know me. My temptation can be to

> Once a group is
> focused on the goodness of
> God and on living in meaningful
> relationship with each
> other, they can do
> great things.

think leadership means casting a spellbinding vision and having people ask how high they should jump. But that's not the way it goes. Because in the trenches and in the pews, people are wondering, *Who is this person and why does he or she want to do this?* The need for relationship and trust is basic.

But once a group is focused on the goodness of God and on living in meaningful relationship with each other, they can do great things. People's lives are changed. The hungry are fed. The poor are cared for. The business and its workers thrive. And a little bit of God's kingdom gets planted and grows here on earth.

The Benefits of
Staying on Mission

We've looked at the negative consequences of succumbing to a shadow mission. There's dissatisfaction, restlessness, boredom. At its worst there's scandal or even death. But what does life look like if we successfully battle our shadow missions? What might our teams achieve if we are able to stay on mission? Is life suddenly rosy?

The surprising answer is: not necessarily. Your life may actually get harder. Not in a destructive way, not in a negative way. But you might discover there's a lot of work to be done. You might need to deal with a certain person. You might have to raise some capital. You might have to make a change that people will criticize. Living on mission doesn't mean your life will be more fun or easier.

But it does mean your attitude will change. Instead of covertly focusing on yourself and the needs of your own ego, you are free to care about your organization. You are able to long for the flourishing of your group, even apart from yourself. I've noticed that when everything is about me—my need to achieve, my need to have success, my need even to survive—the team stumbles. But when I'm able to give up even the need for a good outcome, I can live in freedom.

I'll tell you a story that illustrates this principle of living in freedom. A couple years ago we invited Dallas Willard to speak at our church. After he finished his talk, I walked him out to his car. He had to go to another venue. As we walked, he was just kind of shuffling along, humming this hymn, this goofy hymn . . . not even humming it well.

What struck me was that usually when people finish giving a talk, their next thoughts are, *How'd it go? How did I do? Did I do okay? Did people think it went well?* And if they think it went well, they feel good. Or if they think it went badly, then they start to feel kind of bad. As a speaker, I wrestle with that, and I see it in most folks who speak in public. But with Dallas, it was like watching a kid let go of a helium balloon. The balloon goes up like this . . . and it's gone . . . it's just gone.

I had heard Dallas talk before about the necessity of letting go of outcomes. As leaders, we need to be aware of outcomes, we need to take them seriously and learn from outcomes, but we should not carry the burden of them. Outcomes are in God's hands. We were not meant to carry them. We must not allow outcomes to crush us. But hearing Dallas talk about letting go of outcomes is one thing. To watch him give a talk and then just let it go . . . it was remarkable.

I've noticed that when everything is about me—my need to achieve, my need to have success, my need even to survive—the team stumbles.

I'd love to have that kind of freedom. But there would be a loss in having it. Because I would have to let go of the narcotic of living off of the applause when something goes well. And I would have to humble myself to realize that I'm part of something far greater than myself.

God's Great Mission

Here is the great news: our little missions are part of a *much bigger* mission. They are part of God's great mission that has been sealed by something far more powerful than our gifts or even our character.

Just look at what was going on behind the scenes in the book of Esther. Esther, as you may know, is the only book in the Old Testament that never mentions God, but in reality he's the main character in the story.

There is a law that's unalterable in this story. There is a will that will not be turned, but it ain't the law of the Medes or the Persians. How is it that, of all the women in the empire, a young Jewish woman named

> Here is the great news:
> our little missions
> are part of a *much
> bigger* mission.

Esther becomes queen? How is it that, of all the people
in the empire, Mordecai should be the one who saves the
king from an assassination plot? How is it that the king
should have insomnia on the very night that Haman builds
a gallows for Mordecai—that of all the stories, the one
read to the king was the one of Mordecai saving his life?
How is it that Haman, the scheming murderer, becomes
the victim of his own schemes, and Mordecai, his intended
victim, becomes instead his replacement? How is it that the
king's ring, given to Haman, ends up on Mordecai's finger?
How did the noose intended for Mordecai end up around

Haman's neck? How is it that the people who marked the Jews for destruction are themselves destroyed?

The writer wants us to know that even in exile, as God's people were then—with no Jerusalem, no temple, no Sanhedrin—God is present. Unseen, unnamed, he is at work behind the scenes, and his purpose is certain.

You can die to your shadow mission and lead with joyful freedom because God is always at work in and around you in unseen, unknown, unnamed, and unlikely ways. He's in a manger, in a desert, on a cross. He's at work behind the scenes in wars and famines and

You can die to your shadow mission and lead with joyful freedom because God is always at work in and around you in unseen, unknown, unnamed, and unlikely ways.

floods and disasters. He is present in both dictatorships and democracies. And he's got his hand on churches, businesses, organizations, and individuals everywhere. God wants to use you *because of* what you do (your mission), but—as Samson shows us—he will also use you *in spite of* what you do. He can turn even your shadow mission into something he can use to his glory and the coming of his kingdom here on earth.

Does this mean we can indulge our shadow mission with impunity? Of course not. As Paul wrote, "What shall we say, then? Shall we go on sinning so that grace may increase? By no means! We are those who have died to sin; how can we live in it any longer?" (Romans 6:1–2). Instead, Paul instructs us, "Offer yourselves to God . . . as an instrument of righteousness" (Romans 6:13). At one time we might have been slaves to our shadow missions, our shameful desires for fame, fortune, power, pleasure, or security. But now we can become servants of

God, increasingly desiring his kind of life and active in his mission for the world.

Not a shadow mission. Just a simple, daily, humble, stretching, joyful peace that you and I can call each other to in the work of him who is light, in whom there is no darkness.

Who knows but that you have come to your position for such a time as this.

ACKNOWLEDGMENTS

A few thank-yous are in order for a project I might otherwise have never thought of. I am grateful to Christine Anderson for overseeing the manuscript and marching it to publication with her typical professionalism and flair. Lori Vanden Bosch did much of the work of synthesizing the initial draft, and Jane Haradine brought polish to the text.

I am also grateful to Jimmy Mellado for the invitation to give the talk that led to this little book, and more than that for his suggestions and encouragement around the content, and more than that for a friendship of many years that is a joy to me. It is a gift to be able to partner with the Willow Creek Association.

LEADERSHIP DEVELOPMENT MATTERS

The Leadership Summit, a two-day event, convenes every August in the Chicago area and is satellite broadcast live to more than 135 locations across North America. Designed for leaders in any arena—ministry, business, nonprofit—its purpose is to encourage and equip Christian leaders with an injection of vision, skill development, and inspiration.

For up-to-date information about The Leadership Summit, visit www.willowcreek.com/summit

When Leadership and Discipleship Collide

Bill Hybels

What do you do when the laws of leadership collide with the teachings of Christ?

Modern business practice and scholarship have honed the laws of leadership. To achieve success, you're supposed to—among other things—leverage your time, choose a strong team and avoid unnecessary controversy. But what happens when the laws of leadership and discipleship collide?

Using stories from his own life and ministry, Bill Hybels shows how the laws of leadership sometimes crash headlong into the demands of discipleship. And how the decisions you make at that point could affect not only you, but the destiny of those you lead.

Hardcover: 978-0-310-28306-5

Making Vision Stick

Andy Stanley

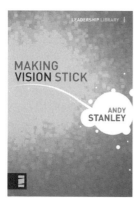

Vision is the lifeblood of your organization.

It should be coursing through the minds and hearts of those you lead, focusing their creativity and galvanizing their efforts. Together, you and your team will strive to make your vision a reality.

But in order for that to happen, you've got to make your vision stick. That's your responsibility as the leader.

Pastor and author Andy Stanley first shows you the reasons why vision doesn't stick. Then, sharing vivid firsthand examples, he walks you through five simple but powerful ways to make your vision infiltrate the hearts, minds, and lives of those you lead.

Making Vision Stick provides the keys you need to propel your organization forward.

Hardcover: 978-0-310-28305-8

Pick up a copy today at your favorite bookstore!

Leading Character

Dan B. Allender

What would it mean for you to reveal your true character to those you lead?

Most would agree that character plays a critical role in leadership. But does that mean the best leaders are nearly perfect people? Or are leaders those who recognize their weaknesses and allow those shortcomings to be transformed into strengths?

Author and speaker Dan Allender draws on humor, real-life stories, and biblical truth to argue that every leader must both *have* a character and *be* a character. How can we proclaim resurrection without naming death and darkness? Likewise, how can we be renewed and restored without acknowledging the reality that we are marred?

"It is in our brokenness," he concludes, "that we have our greatest opportunity to reveal the heart of God's goodness." And the greatest opportunity to enhance and strengthen our leadership.

Hardcover: 978-0-310-28762-9

Pick up a copy today at your favorite bookstore!

Willow Creek Association

Vision, Training, Resources for Prevailing Churches

This resource was created to serve you and to help you build a local church that prevails. It is just one of many ministry tools that are part of the Willow Creek Resources® line, published by the Willow Creek Association together with Zondervan.

The Willow Creek Association (WCA) was created in 1992 to serve a rapidly growing number of churches from across the denominational spectrum that are committed to helping unchurched people become fully-devoted followers of Christ. Membership in the WCA now numbers over 12,000 Member Churches worldwide from more than ninety denominations.

The Willow Creek Association links like-minded Christian leaders with each other and with strategic vision, training and resources in order to help them build prevailing churches designed to reach their redemptive potential. Here are some of the ways the WCA does that.

The Leadership Summit—A once a year, two-day learning experience to envision and equip Christians with leadership gifts and responsibilities. Presented live on Willow's campus as well as via satellite simulcast to over 135 locations across North America—plus more than eighty international cities feature the Summit by way of videocast every Fall—this event is designed to increase the leadership effectiveness of pastors, ministry staff, volunteer church leaders and Christians in the marketplace.

Ministry-Specific Conferences—Throughout the year the WCA hosts a variety of conferences and training events—both at Willow Creek's main campus and offsite, across North America and around the world. These events are for church leaders and volunteers in areas such as group life, children's ministry, student ministry, preaching and teaching, the arts and stewardship.

Willow Creek Resources®—Provides churches with trusted and field-tested ministry resources on important topics such as leadership, volunteer ministries, spiritual formation, stewardship, evangelism, group life, children's ministry, student ministry, the arts and more.

WCA Member Benefits—Includes substantial discounts to WCA training events, a 20 percent discount on all Willow Creek Resources®, *Defining Moments* monthly audio journal for leaders, quarterly *Willow* magazine, access to a Members-Only section on WCA's web site, monthly communications and more. Member Churches also receive special discounts and premier services through the WCA's growing number of ministry partners—Select Service Providers—and save an average of $500 annually depending on the level of engagement.

For specific information about WCA conferences, resources, membership, and other ministry services, contact:

Willow Creek Association
P.O. Box 3188, Barrington, IL 60011-3188
Phone: 847-570-9812 • Fax: 847-765-5046
www.willowcreek.com

Share Your Thoughts

With the Author: Your comments will be forwarded to the author when you send them to *zauthor@zondervan.com*.

With Zondervan: Submit your review of this book by writing to *zreview@zondervan.com*.

Free Online Resources at
www.zondervan.com/hello

 Zondervan AuthorTracker: Be notified whenever your favorite authors publish new books, go on tour, or post an update about what's happening in their lives.

 Daily Bible Verses and Devotions: Enrich your life with daily Bible verses or devotions that help you start every morning focused on God.

 Free Email Publications: Sign up for newsletters on fiction, Christian living, church ministry, parenting, and more.

 Zondervan Bible Search: Find and compare Bible passages in a variety of translations at www.zondervanbiblesearch.com.

 Other Benefits: Register yourself to receive online benefits like coupons and special offers, or to participate in research.